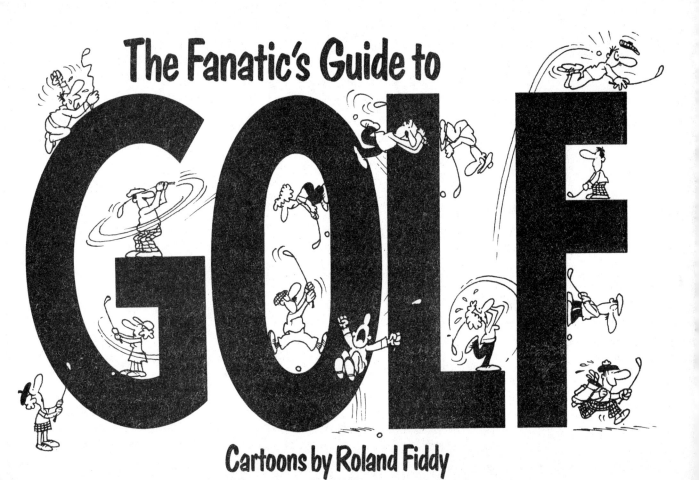

# The Fanatic's Guide to GOLF

## Cartoons by Roland Fiddy

**In the same series:**
*The Fanatic's Guide to Sex*

Published in Great Britain in 1989 by Exley Publications Ltd,
16 Chalk Hill, Watford, Herts WD1 4BN, United Kingdom.
Second and third printings 1989

**ISBN 1-85015-172-5**

Typeset by Brush Off Studios, St Albans, Herts AL3 4PH.
Printed and bound in Great Britain by
The Guernsey Press Co. Ltd, Guernsey, Channel Islands.

# Roland Fiddy

Born in Plymouth, Devon in 1941. Studied
at the West of England College of Art
Bristol. Works as a freelance
cartoonist and illustrator. His cartoons
have been published in Britain, the
United States and many other countries.
Has taken part in International Cartoon
Festivals since 1984, and has won
the following awards:

| | | | |
|---|---|---|---|
| 1984 | First Prize, | Beringen, | Belgium |
| 1984 | Special Prize, | Tokyo, | Japan |
| 1984 | Public Prize, | Amsterdam, | Holland. |
| 1985 | First Prize, | Amsterdam, | Holland. |
| 1985 | Second Prize, | Knokke Heist, | Belgium. |
| 1986 | First Prize, | Beringen, | Belgium. |
| 1986 | First Prize | Amsterdam, | Holland. |
| 1986 | First Prize | Sofia, | Bulgaria |
| 1987 | Second Prize | Skopje, | Yugoslavia. |
| 1987 | Casino Prize, | Knokke Heist, | Belgium |
| 1987 | UNESCO Prize | Gabrovo | Bulgaria |
| 1987 | First Prize | Piracicaba, | Brazil |
| 1988 | Golden Date | Bordighera | Italy |
| 1988 | Second Prize | London | England |
| 1989 | E.E.C. Prize | Kruishoutem | Belgium |

*Golf: how it all began ...*

2

*... and how it continued.*

*Golf is not only recreational ...*
*... it is also useful.*

*The fanatical golfer addressing the ball.*

The fanatical golfer should not worry about his standard of play, as this will affect his standard of play.

*Nothing must interfere with his concentration.*

*The fanatical golfer never misses an opportunity to improve his...*

*... er – or her putting.*

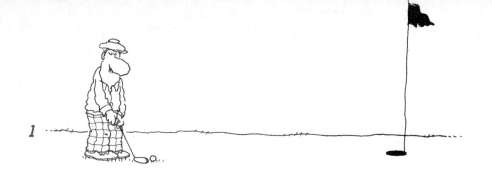

La Ronde

*The fanatical golfer knows how important it is to present a brave face.*

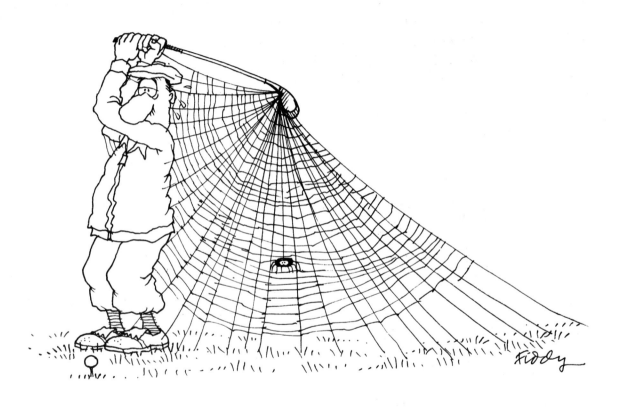

*The fanatical golfer knows how important it is not to rush the back swing.*

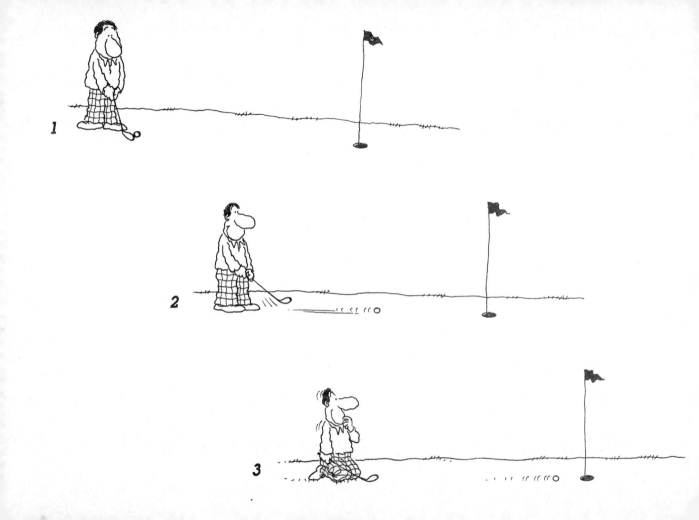

**1**

**2**

**3**

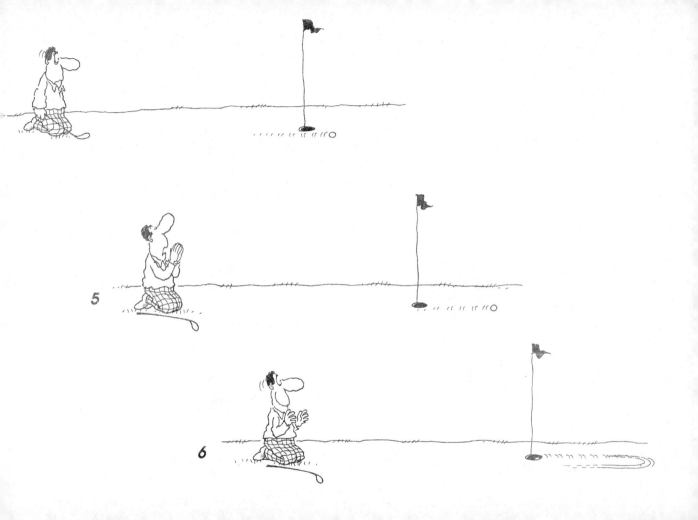

OH, THAT! I DON'T KNOW— IT JUST APPEARS AS SOON AS I GET ON A GOLF COURSE!
Fiddy

*1*

You must not carry more than fourteen clubs in your bag ...

2

*... this is a sensible rule for obvious reasons.*

*Play the ball as it lies.*

*This is against the Rules ...*

*... and so is this.*

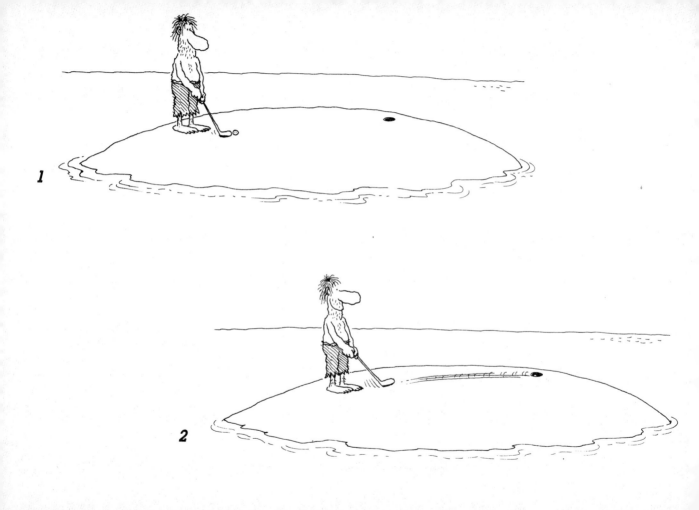

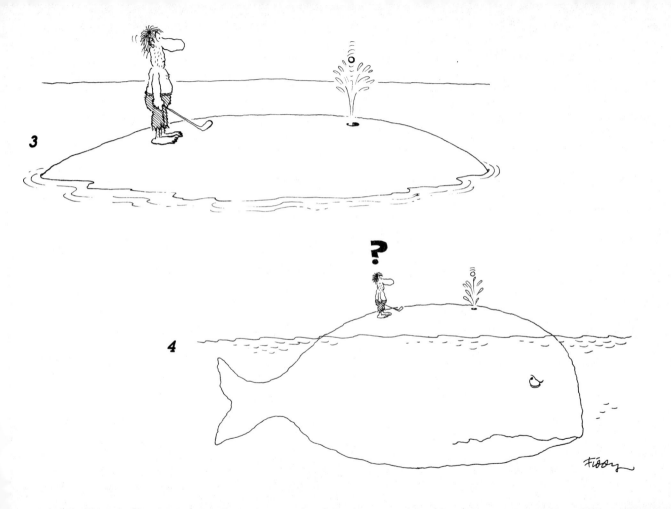

*Fanatical golfers need to be specially patient with beginners...*

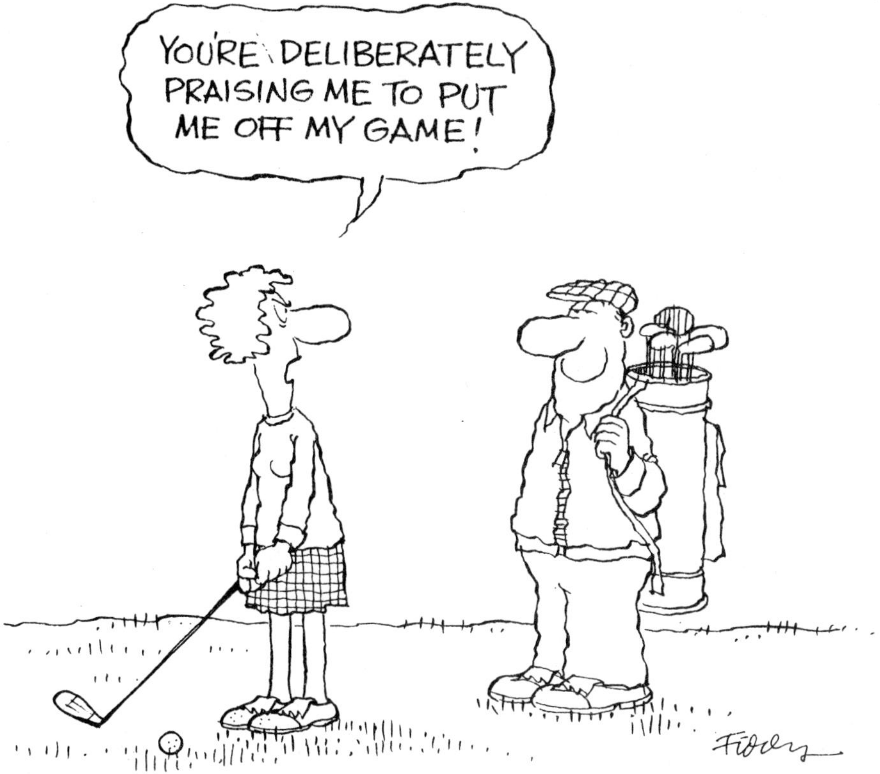
YOU'RE DELIBERATELY PRAISING ME TO PUT ME OFF MY GAME!
Fiddy

"Old men forget; yet all shall be forgot,
But he'll remember with advantages,
What feats he did that day ..."

(Shakespeare: _Henry V_)

*To the fanatical golfer, every difficult hole is another Everest to conquer.*

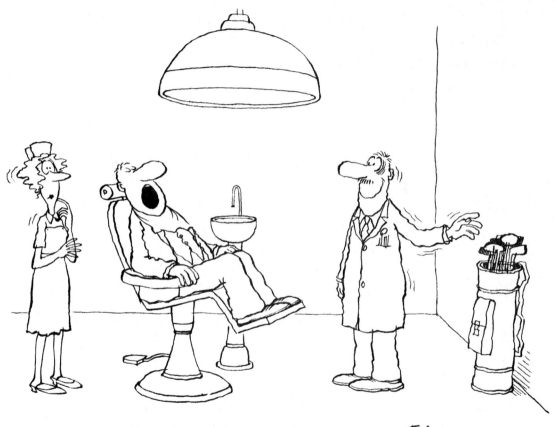

*The fanatical golfer finds it hard to accept criticism ...*

3

*... or to ignore it ...*

*but is willing to take constructive advice.*

1

2

3

4

*The fanatical golfer understands the importance ...*

*... of controlling one's temperament.*

*The game is full of surprises.*

*Of course, not everybody appreciates golf –
some people think it's just a load of balls.*

*The angler and the golfer swopping stories.*

*Golf: the ideal combination of recreation and exercise.*

Other fun giftbooks from Exley Publications:

In the same series: **The Fanatic's Guide to Sex** also by Roland Fiddy: £2.99 (paperback). Now this is one that you won't give Aunt Matilda for Christmas — unless she's really liberated! On the other hand, your lover, your husband or wife, your (selected) friends and some of your family will find it hilarious and in moderately good taste....

**The Illustrated Golf Address Book** £6.99 including VAT (hardback). New from Exley Publications is this superb series of full-colour address books, elegantly bound with picture covers, with generous address spaces. Artists featured include Van Gogh, Monet, Breughel, Stubbs, F. Gordon Crosbie and "Spy". The series includes: Flower-Arranging, Gardening, Horses, Motoring, Sailing, Tea and Wine.

Also available are the **Illustrated Flower-Arranging Day Book,** the **Illustrated Gardening Day book** and the **Illustrated Wine Day Book.** These dateless diaries have 52 full colour pictures (one for each full week of the year). £8.99 (including VAT, hardback).

**The Crazy World of Golf** £3.99 (hardback). Over eighty hilarious cartoons show the really dedicated golfer in his (or her) every absurdity. What really goes on on the course, and the golfer's life when not playing, are chronicled in loving detail.

There are now 15 other titles in this best-selling cartoon series — one of them must be right for a friend of yours....

The Crazy World of Birdwatching (Peter Rigby)
The Crazy World of Cats (Bill Stott)
The Crazy World of Gardening (Bill Stott)
The Crazy World of the Handyman
     (Roland Fiddy)
The Crazy World of Jogging (David Pye)
The Crazy World of Love (Roland Fiddy)
The Crazy World of Marriage (Bill Stott)
The Crazy World of Music (Bill Stott)
The Crazy World of the Office (Bill Stott)
The Crazy World of Photography (Bill Stott)
The Crazy World of Rugby (Bill Stott)
The Crazy World of Sailing (Peter Rigby)
The Crazy World of Sex (David Pye)
The Crazy World of Skiing
     (Craig Peterson & Jerry Emerson)
The Crazy World of Tennis (Peter Rigby)

These books make super presents. Order them from your local bookseller or from Exley Publications Ltd, Dept BP, 16 Chalk Hill, Watford, Herts WD1 4BN. (Please send £1.00 to cover post and packing.) Exley Publications reserves the right to show new retail prices on books which may vary from those previously advertised.